RITCHIE VALENS™
Songbook *Hits and B-Sides*
by Ryan Sheeler

T0088819

To access audio, visit:
www.HalLeonard.com/MyLibrary
Enter Code
1835-7687-6516-4715

Edited by Ronny S. Schiff

CENTERSTREAM®

All rights for publication and distribution are reserved.

RITCHIE VALENS
Songbook *Hits and B-Sides*

Edited by Ronny S. Schiff

Graphic Design and Typesetting by Charylu Roberts / O.Ruby Productions

Cover Design by James Creative Group

ISBN 978-1-57424-408-3

Published by Centerstream Publishing,
P.O. Box 17878
Anaheim Hills, CA 92817
714.779-9390
www.centerstream-usa.com
centerstrm@aol.com

Distributed Worldwide by Hal Leonard LLC

EXCLUSIVELY DISTRIBUTED BY

7777 W. BLUEMOUND RD. P.O. BOX 13819 MILWAUKEE, WI 53213

Table of Contents

Songs

Note: the transcription to "La Bamba" can be found in *Ritchie Valens: His Guitars and Music* by Ryan Sheeler (also available through Centerstream Publishing / Hal Leonard LLC)

Introduction

I have been a fan of Ritchie Valens' music for a long time. My parents introduced me to "oldies" music (their generation's music) in the 1970s and early 1980s. There were great radio stations based out of Des Moines, Iowa, such as KSO, KRNT, and KIOA. And when the 1987 film *La Bamba* was released, I loved it. The accompanying soundtrack with Los Lobos performing Ritchie's songs remains my favorite movie soundtrack to this day.

In my first book on Ritchie, *Ritchie Valens: His Guitars and Music* (Centerstream Publications, 2019), I delved into Ritchie's guitar collection, playing styles, musical history, and also offered a new transcription of "La Bamba." In this second book, I continue with transcriptions of all of the rest of Ritchie's hits, B-sides, and commemorative singles issues by Del-Fi in the years 1958–1960.

With these new transcriptions, I strived to be faithful to the recordings and bring the songs into the modern realm for contemporary musicians. For many of the songs, I extracted the famous guitar intros, fills and solos. There are notes for each of the songs that include some of the history behind the songs and some analysis.

In his brief eight-month career, Ritchie left us with two studio albums, one live album, and a host of outtakes and demos. In these musical snapshots, we catch a glimpse of a meteoric talent that had just begun to shine, before being cut short far too soon. We now have the benefit of history and hindsight, but suffice to say, that Ritchie blazed a trail of innovation that is still being mined and felt today all over the world. We are thankful for Ritchie, his music, and his legacy. We cherish the music and the memories, we celebrate his life, and remember the joy he gave us.

Ryan Sheeler

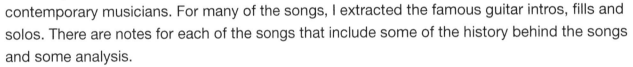

Song Notes and Transcriptions

There are a few fine biographies of Ritchie Valens in various books (the best is Beverly Mendheim's excellent *Ritchie Valens: The First Latino Rocker*—hers was the first full-length biography about Ritchie). I have corresponded at-length with Beverly about Ritchie and his guitars for this project, and she has been very gracious in helping me with this project. As any musician, historian, or musicologist will tell you, music (or any art for that matter) does not exist in a vacuum. It is best to not separate the study of art from the culture in which it was created. Music is not only the product of God-given talent, nurturing and hard work, but it is also a product of the environment and of the times.

Ritchie Valens had only two albums, *Ritchie Valens* and *Ritchie*, both released after his death in 1959. In reality, there were only one-and-a-half studio albums, as his second album was comprised partially of the remaining finished studio tracks and filled with some cleaned-up demos for the balance. Ritchie's recording sessions were done mostly at Gold Star Studios in Los Angeles and also at Bob Keane's home studio. Keane put together a stellar band of musicians to back up Ritchie. Several of these names, of course, are very familiar to many:

First promo photo, summer 1958

Pacoima Jr. High Concert: Ritchie with drummer Don Phillips; live at Pacoima Junior High performance, December 10, 1958

- René Hall—guitar and Danelectro ("Dano" Longhorn 6-string bass)

- Carol Kaye—guitar

- Red Callender and/or Buddy Clark—upright bass

- Earl Palmer—drums

The Singles

Year	A-Side	B-Side	Label	Album	Additional Info
1958	Come On, Let's Go	Framed	Del-Fi 4106	*Ritchie Valens*	
1958	Donna	La Bamba	Del-Fi 4110	*Ritchie Valens*	
1959	Fast Freight	Big Baby Blues	Del-Fi 4111	*Ritchie*	as "Arvee Allens"; later pressings shown as "Ritchie Valens"
1959	That's My Little Suzie	In a Turkish Town	Del-Fi 4114	*Ritchie Valens*	
1959	Little Girl	We Belong Together (from *Ritchie Valens*)	Del-Fi 4117	*Ritchie*	Issued on gold Valens Memorial Series abels. Del-Fi 4117 was also issued with picture sleeve.
1959	Stay Beside Me	Big Baby Blues	Del-Fi 4128	*Ritchie*	Issued on gold Valens Memorial Series labels.
1960	The Paddi-Wack Song	Cry, Cry, Cry	Del-Fi 4133	*Ritchie*	Issued on gold Valens Memorial Series labels.

"Come On, Let's Go" is Ritchie's first big hit single—the song that put him "on the map." It was his first single, released on Del-Fi circa June 1958. The hook of the song comes from the phrase "Come on let's go," which is something that Ritchie's mom and family used to say a lot around the Valenzuela household. The song features the rock-solid grooves of drummer Earl Palmer, bassist Buddy Clark, and René Hall on Danelectro six-string bass, with Carol Kaye on extra rhythm guitar. Producer Bob Keane supposedly had to make more than forty tape edits for the song, to help capture and correct the meter of the song, because Ritchie never really sang it the same way from take to take. The song is in classic AABA form.

The guitar solo and fills for "Come On, Let's Go" were also played by René Hall in this particular case (Ritchie did many of his own guitar solos on his other songs). The solo features some nice bends and grace notes. Hall uses the A minor/blues pentatonic scale with added major 6th note implying a Dorian/blues hybrid (A-C-C♯-D-D♯/E♭-E-F♯-G), and the A major pentatonic scale (A-B-C♯-E-F♯), often shifting between the two with fingering position shifts, bends and slides. The solo begins and ends with the "blues box"-fingering of A minor pentatonic on the 8th fret.

"Framed" was the B-side of "Come On, Let's Go" and is a cover of a 1954 song written by Jerry Leiber and Mike Stoller. The song was originally done by doo-wop/R&B group, The Robins, of which two members went on to become The Coasters. Ritchie's version, recorded in the summer of 1958, is the first cover version. A cool one-bar riff anchors the tune, and Ritchie plays a few quick, tasty lead guitar solos between the chorus and verses. The song is basically a modified or elongated blues form in the key of G. Be aware that the verses are mostly spoken/sung; I tried to approximate the pitches and timing. Note also the shifting meters between 12/8 and 6/8, which could equate to 4/4 and 2/4 time with triplets.

The guitar fills, and solo are a blend of G major (G-A-B-C-D-E-F♯) and G minor pentatonic/blues (G-B♭(B)-C-C♯-D-F). The main riff in G blues is a standard blues maneuver found in dozens of blues tunes in the in the postwar period of electric/urban blues, like those of T-Bone Walker, Muddy Waters, Howlin' Wolf, Lowell Fulson, Chuck Berry and many others. The song itself is in an extended 16-bar blues form (extra four bars of the I chord at the beginning of each section/chorus of the form).

"Donna" is the second of the three signature Ritchie Valens songs, and is truly one of the great ballads of the first rock era. As is the story, Ritchie wanted to write a song for his girlfriend Donna Ludwig. He had the opening hook "I had a girl and Donna was her name" and Bob Keane helped him flesh out the song. Beverly Mendheim's book offers several possible scenarios for the song's creation. The song is in classic AABA form. I notated the chart in F major, but one could also capo on the first fret and play the song with E-chord fingering and it is possible that Ritchie could have done it that way. Using the capo would shorten the string, and, in this case, would sound an F chord with an open E fingering, thus using open strings to have a slightly fuller sound than barring with the finger across all the strings.

"Donna" backed with "La Bamba" * was Ritchie's biggest hit, reaching #2 on the *Billboard* charts. It was released by Del-Fi in October of 1958.

The guitar solo and fills to "Donna" utilize primarily the F major scale (F-G-A-B♭-C-D-E-F) with a brief allusion to F minor pentatonic (F-A♭-B♭-C) at the end of the bridge section. Several things to notice:

- How Ritchie's guitar fills follow the vocal melody—he always played and sang at the same time in the studio
- How Ritchie's guitar fills target dissonant notes—especially the major 2nd (G) and major 7th (E)
- Substantial use of grace notes (can be played as hammer-on slurs)
- There are less fills on Verse 3—and they use the material from the Verse 1 fills

* *Note: the transcription to "La Bamba" can be found my other Ritchie Valens book*
  Ritchie Valens: His Guitars and Music *(available through Centerstream Publishing / Hal Leonard LLC)*

"Fast Freight" is often thought of as the first "surf" song and it is easy to see why. The riffs here bear the strong influence of Dick Dale, who knew and "mentored" Ritchie at various times and gigs throughout Southern California. A strong Eddie Cochran influence is present here as well. This tune has a fast rock groove and some great pentatonic blues licks by Ritchie. And notice the heavy reverb and echo on the guitar here, something that foreshadows the imminent surf rock and instrumental rock trends that would come into the mainstream just a very short while later. "Fast Freight" with the B-side of "Big Baby Blues" was released as a Del-Fi single in December 1958, under the pseudonym of "Arvee Allens."

"Big Baby Blues" shows Ritchie's affinity and natural talent for the blues with his classic blues guitar playing. There are some great blues licks by Ritchie throughout—including some rapid-fire pentatonic passages, and some tasty bends, ghost bends, slides and grace notes. Since this is a guitar solo score, I notated this one in standard treble clef. As you know, guitar is a transposing instrument written up an octave or sounding down an octave. So, the guitarist would read the notes in a treble clef as normal, but the resulting pitch would sound down an octave from standard concert pitch. "Big Baby Blues" was the B-side of "Fast Freight," released in December 1958, again, under the pseudonym of "Arvee Allens."

"That's My Little Suzie" is a catchy little number that Ritchie wrote for a neighbor girl. It is a great example of Ritchie's ability and talent for combining some of his own sounds, heritage, and feel into a catchy, driving rock song. Note the Mexican flavor of the opening riff and how Ritchie uses it with the rock beat.

In the guitar solo for "…Suzie," Ritchie uses some very cool pre-bend (ghost bend) and release figures, as well as some nice pull-offs, and concludes the solo with some descending double-stops that help to enhance the Mexican flavor. The solo segues directly back into the main riff to finish out the 12-bar phrase.

"In a Turkish Town" shows again that Ritchie was capable of writing and singing great ballads ("Donna"). "…Turkish Town" is a unique song in several respects: First, Ritchie uses a distinctive echo/tremolo effect on his guitar on the intro and solo, which enriches the Middle Eastern effect of the song. This was likely some amp tremolo (like on a Fender or Magnatone amp) and enhanced by the famous echo chamber at Gold Star Studios—the same one where Phil Spector would make his famous "Wall of Sound" recordings just a few short years later. Second, there are several meter shifts from 4/4, to 5/4, to 3/4 time in the song. This may be a combination of several factors—either how Ritchie played it that way, or the result of some judicious editing. Either way, the result is a wonderful, hidden gem in Ritchie's short recorded output.

The guitar solo for "…Turkish Town" is simple yet effective. The same ambient echo effect used in the rhythm guitar track is present here also. The solo utilizes the standard E-major arpeggio in open position (E-G♯-B), along with the upper-neighbor tone of C♯, which helps imply the chord change to A (A-C♯-E; IV chord in E). The last phrase of the solo features a G-natural in a brief nod to the E minor pentatonic scale for some blues flavor (E-G-A-B-D).

"Little Girl" is credited to both Ritchie and Bob Keane—a nice mid-tempo slow dance song. It was released as a single on Del-Fi in July 1959, with "We Belong Together" as the B-side. The song is AABABA (32-bar pop with extra bridge and verse) form. Guitar-wise not much noteworthy here, but René Hall's Dano bass makes another appearance with the main riff and doubles the other bass. Interesting "on-the-fly" modulation happens at the very end where the last verse/tag (Verse 3a—repeat of the "A" section) modulates up a whole-step from A to B major, without much warning or preparation at all. Only a E/F♯ chord (or F♯11–F♯ dominant 11th: F♯-E-G♯-B, low-to-high) is the setup chord and that comes very quickly and is barely heard at all. A nice jazz/blues maneuver ends the song with the chromatic C to B chords.

"We Belong Together" is another great ballad in Ritchie's repertoire (in addition to "Donna" and "Stay Beside Me") that shows his considerable emotional range as a performer. The song is originally from 1958 written and recorded by New York R&B duo Robert (Carr) & Johnny (Mitchell) (with a co-write by Hy Weiss). Prominent features of the song are René Hall's Dano bass work, and Carol Kaye's rhythm guitar.

"Stay Beside Me" is third of Ritchie's famous ballads, along with "Donna" and "We Belong Together," and it is every bit as great a song and performance as the other two. The heavy guitar tremolo first heard in "In a Turkish Town" has returned here. Ritchie's strummed guitar chords with tremolo and with Carol Kaye's steady rhythm behind him, sets up one of Ritchie's most emotional vocal performances that he ever committed to record. It was released as a single by Del-Fi in November 1959, after Ritchie's death.

"The Paddi-Wack Song" is Ritchie's rocked-up arrangement of the old and very well-known children's nursery rhyme. As noted in the liner notes of the Ritchie album—Bob Keane persuaded Ritchie to record the song easing Ritchie's initial reticence about recording a "nursery rhyme" But Keane's instincts again proved to be right—Ritchie adapted to the song into his own style and hard-driving rhythm and the result is a very fun ride. The song is a combination of strophic 8-bar phrases of lyrics ("This old man, he played ____"), over the top of differing 8-bar phrases of music; almost like verse-refrain form, but not quite. Of note is the fact that Ritchie skips over Verse 3 (there is no "This old man, he played three" in Ritchie's version) for some unknown reason, be it spontaneity or editing. Again, the powerful groove of Earl Palmer's drums and René Hall's Danelectro bass with Buddy Clark's upright, is on full display here, and the energy is palpable. It is possible to use a capo on this song as well; putting the capo on the first fret would allow for open-string fingerings in the key of E major. "The Paddi-Wack Song" was the third of three commemorative singles released by Del-Fi in the 1959–'60 time frame.

The guitar solo for "The Paddi-Wack Song" is a 16-bar phrase. It is curious in that the chord progression rambles between the F and B-flat chords and does not change where you would normally expect it to in blues or pop changes. Ritchie's solo is in F minor pentatonic (F-A♭-B♭-C-E♭-F); again, his use of double-stops and string-bending techniques shows a heavy blues influence.

"Cry, Cry, Cry" is another uptempo rocker; this one is a stylistic hybrid between "That's My Little Suzie" and "Ooh, My Head" with the main guitar riff being slightly reminiscent of "…Suzie." "Cry, Cry, Cry" was the B-Side to the single for "The Paddi-Wack Song," posthumously released by Del-Fi in 1960. The verses are in 12-bar blues in the key of B-flat—and the song features a lot of stop-time with the main riff alternating between the vocal lines. Again, it is entirely possible that Ritchie capoed on the first fret and played the riff with "A" fingerings.

The guitar intro riff to "Cry, Cry, Cry" is in B-flat major pentatonic (B♭-C-D-F-G). But the solo is B-flat minor pentatonic (B♭-D♭-E♭-F-A♭). The solo features a lot of string bending in classic Ritchie fashion and wide interval leaps from the low octave B♭ scale to way up on the 14th and 16th frets, higher on the neck. Aim for a freewheeling type of feel throughout.

Audio Tracks and Notes

In the audio portion of this book, you can listen through two of Ritchie's songs "Come On, Let's Go" and "Donna," along with discussion and performance tracks. We tried to perform these with some of Ritchie's original style and feel, but also with a nod to Los Lobos' versions on the film soundtrack.

For my guitar parts, I am playing a Fender/Warmoth Stratocaster custom with DiMarzio pickups into a Fender Tone Master Deluxe Reverb amp. On the solo for "Come On, Let's Go," I am also using an Xotic EP Booster and Barber Burn Unit overdrive. Tom is playing a Fender Player series Telecaster through a Fender '65 Deluxe Reverb Reissue amp, with an Xotic SP Compressor.

*Ritchie and Bob Keane on
"Pik-A-Platter" TV show, 1958 or 1959*

Track 1: Introduction and "Come On, Let's Go" — notes and discussion with Ryan

Track 2: "Come On, Let's Go" — full song with band

Track 3: "Donna" — notes and discussion with Ryan

Track 4: "Donna" — full song with band

Track 5: Conclusion

> Ryan Sheeler – lead (solos and fills) and rhythm guitar (left)
>
> *With:*
>
> Tom Box – lead and harmony vocals, rhythm guitar (right)
> Scott Draper – bass guitar, piano
> Jim Noxon – drums

Recorded at The Spacement – Ames, Iowa | Engineered by Bryon Dudley | Mastered with Bandlab (*www.bandlab.com*)

Come On, Let's Go

From the album Ritchie Valens *(1959)*

Words and Music by Ritchie Valens
Transcribed by Ryan Sheeler

COME ON, LET'S GO

From the album Ritchie Valens *(1959)*

Words and Music by Ritchie Valens
Transcribed by Ryan Sheeler

1. Intro Riff

Driving Rock with slight swing ♩ = 150

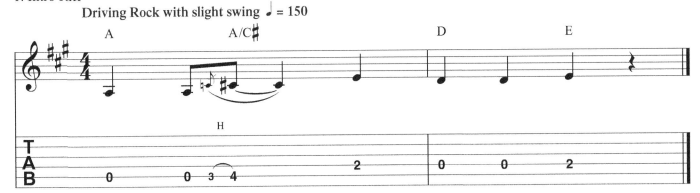

2. Guitar Break (mm.7-8)

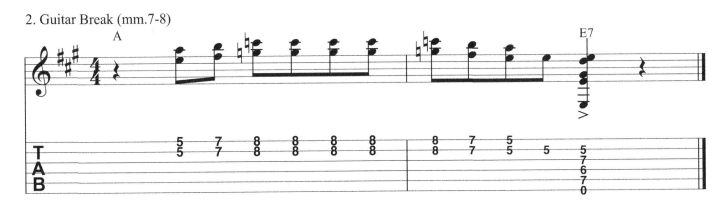

3. Guitar Solo (mm.42-58)

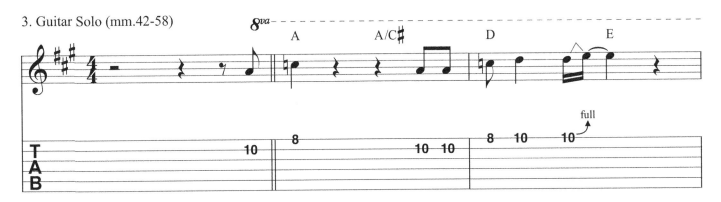

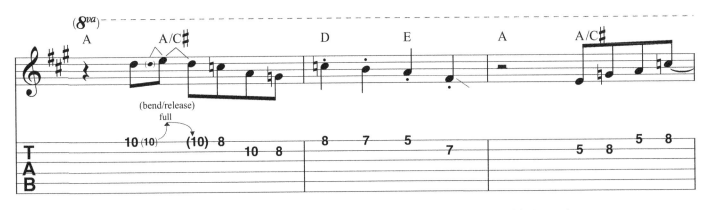

COME ON, LET'S GO

15

FRAMED

From the album Ritchie Valens *(1959)*

Words and Music by Jerry Leiber and Mike Stoller
Transcribed by Ryan Sheeler

Easy Shuffle ♩. = 84

FRAMED

framed.

Verse 2

They took me in the line-up and let those bright lights shine.

There was ten poor souls like me in that line.

I knew I was the vic-tim of some-one's e-vil plan,

when the stool pigeon walked in and said, "There's your man!" I was

Chorus 2

framed, framed, I was blamed.

Framed, framed, framed, well I nev-er do noth-in'

but I al-ways get blamed.

FRAMED

18

Guitar

Framed

From the album Ritchie Valens *(1959)*

Easy Shuffle ♩. = 84

Words and Music by Jerry Leiber and Mike Stoller
Transcribed by Ryan Sheeler

1. Intro/Verse Riff

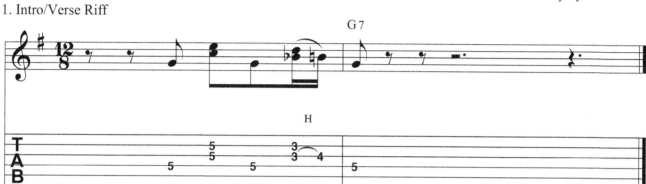

2. Guitar Solo Fill (mm. 33-34)

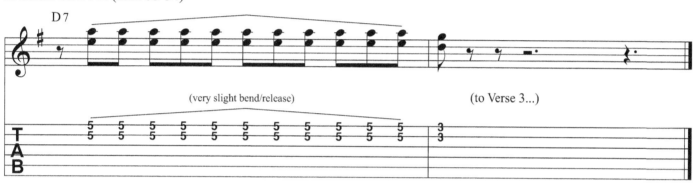

*"Winter Dance Party" stop at the Eagles Ballroom,
Kenosha, Wisconsin, January 24, 1959*

19

Donna

From the album Ritchie Valens *(1959)*

Words and Music by Ritchie Valens
Transcribed by Ryan Sheeler

Alt: Capo on 1st fret, play with
"E" fingerings: down 1/2 step

Intro/Refrain

Ballad ♩. = 66

Oh, Don - na, oh Don - na,

oh Don - na oh Don - na.

𝄋 Verse 1

I had a girl____ and Don - na____ was her name,

since she left me____ I've nev - er____ been the same. 'Cause I

love ____ my ____ girl ____ Don - na, ____ oh ____ where can you

Last time to Coda ⊕

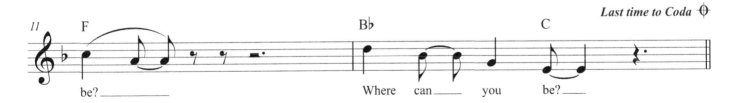

be? ____ Where can ____ you be? ____

Verse 2

Now that you're gone, ____ I'm left all ____ a - lone,

Guitar

DONNA

From the album Ritchie Valens *(1959)*

Words and Music by Ritchie Valens
Transcribed by Ryan Sheeler

1. Verses 1 and 3 - fills

Ballad ♩. = 66

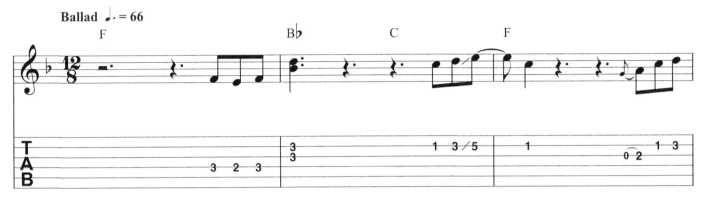

2. Verse 2 - fills

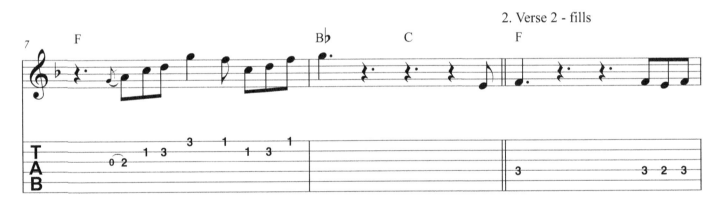

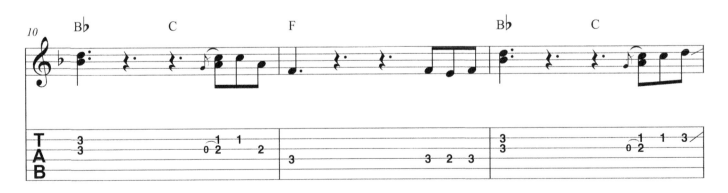

Donna

3. Bridge - fills

4. Guitar Solo

FAST FREIGHT

From the album Ritchie Valens *(1959)*

Words and Music by Ritchie Valens
Transcribed by Ryan Sheeler

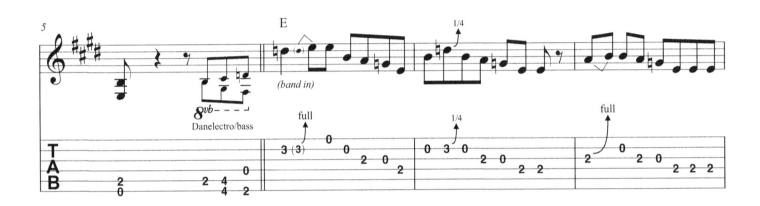

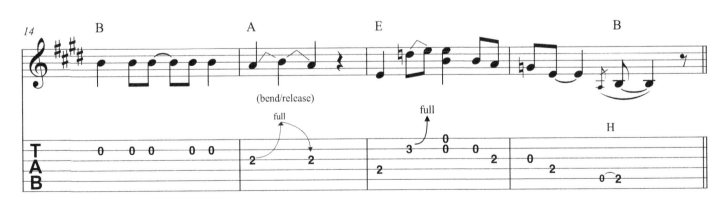

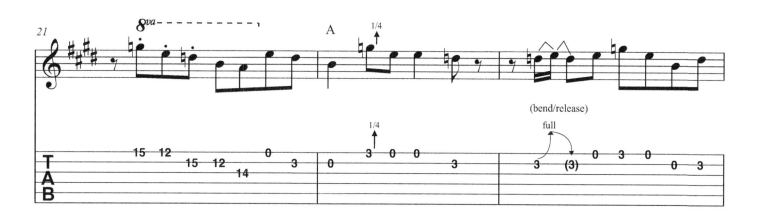

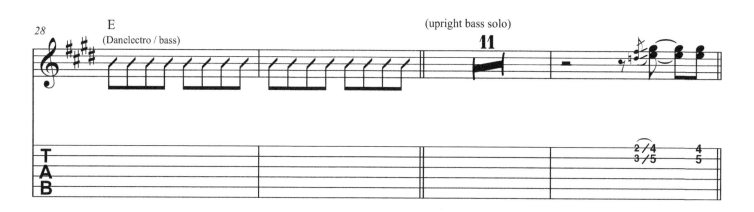

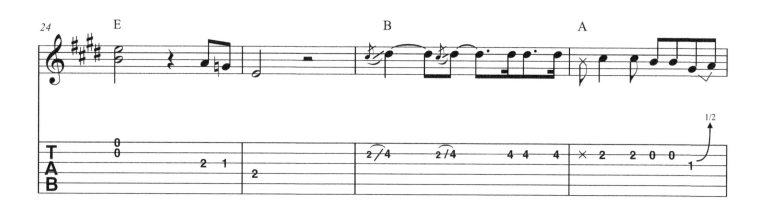

Fast Freight

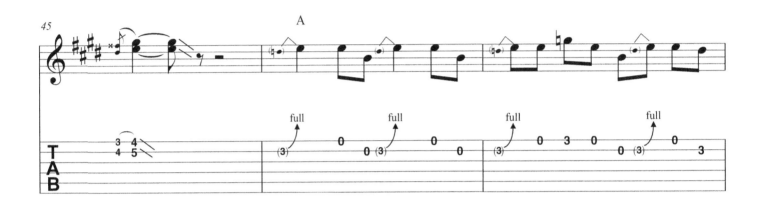

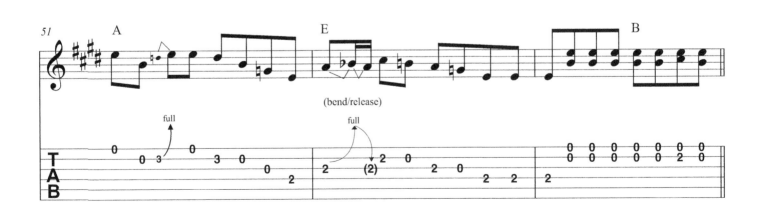

FAST FREIGHT

(gliss.)

full

full

(freely to the end...)

(let ring with reverb and echo)

Guitar

BIG BABY BLUES

From the album Ritchie Valens *(1959)*

Words and Music by Ritchie Valens
Transcribed by Ryan Sheeler

Big Baby Blues

Big Baby Blues

That's My Little Suzie

From the album Ritchie Valens *(1959)*

Words and Music by Ritchie Valens and Robert Kuhn
Transcribed by Ryan Sheeler

Latin Rock feel ♩ = 138

(gtr riff)

Verse 1

I got a gal named ___ Su - zie, she knows just what to ___ do, she's just a rock - in', she knows what to do. ___

Verse 2

(band out) *(band in)* She knows how to love me ___ and rock it too, ___ that's my lit - tle Su - zie, *(band hit)* she knows what to do. ___

𝄋 Bridge

(w/intro riff) *(band walk-up)* ___ She rocks to the left and she rocks to the right, she

Guitar

Alt: Capo on 3rd fret;
use "E" fingerings

THAT'S MY LITTLE SUZIE

From the album Ritchie Valens *(1959)*

Words and Music by Ritchie Valens and Robert Kuhn
Transcribed by Ryan Sheeler

1. Main Riff – 3rd position

2. Main Riff – open position (alt)

3. Main Riff – capo on 3rd fret for key of G; using "E" fingerings

4. Guitar Solo (mm. 36-48 in chart)

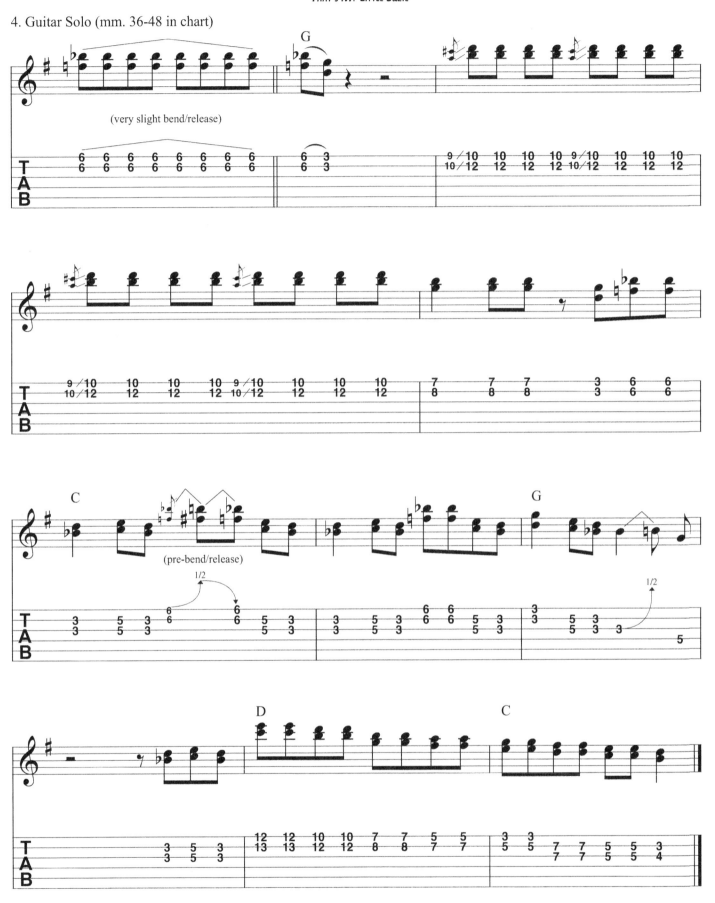

In a Turkish Town

From the album Ritchie Valens *(1959)*

Words and Music by Ritchie Valens
Transcribed by Ryan Sheeler

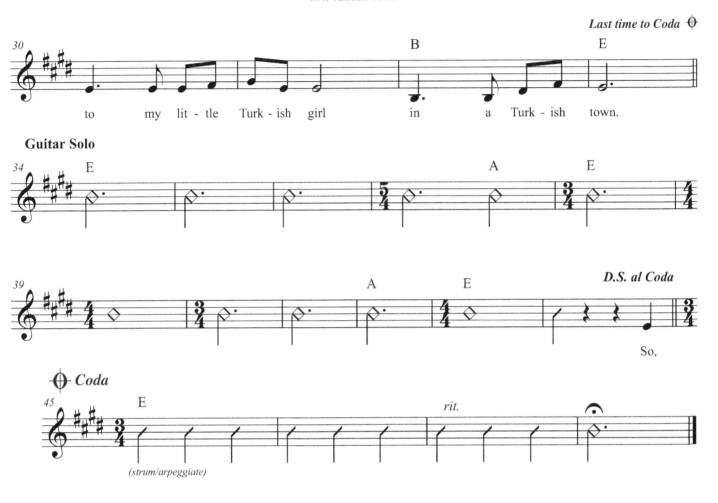

Last time to Coda

Guitar Solo

D.S. al Coda

So,

Coda

rit.

(strum/arpeggiate)

Ritchie professional promo photo, January 1959

In a Turkish Town

From the album Ritchie Valens *(1959)*

Words and Music by Ritchie Valens
Transcribed by Ryan Sheeler

1. Guitar Intro

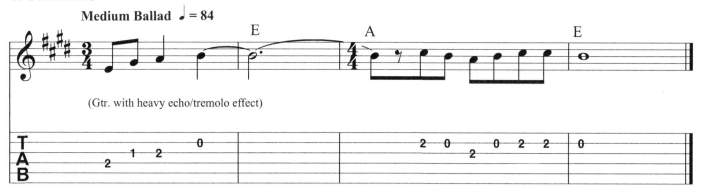

(Gtr. with heavy echo/tremolo effect)

2. Guitar Solo (mm. 34-44 in chart)

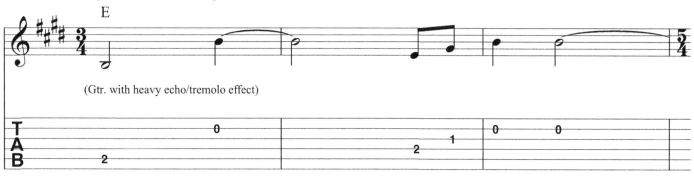

(Gtr. with heavy echo/tremolo effect)

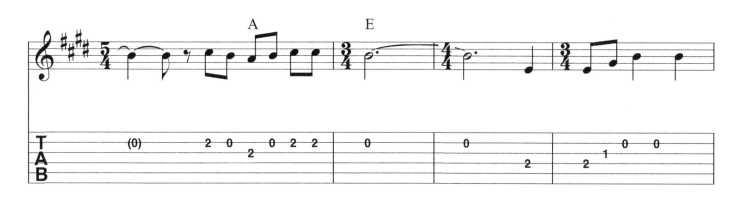

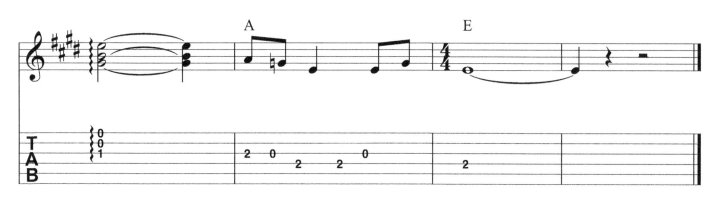

Little Girl

From the album Ritchie (1959)

Words and Music by Ritchie Valens and Robert Kuhn
Transcribed by Ryan Sheeler

LITTLE GIRL

From the album Ritchie *(1959)*

Words and Music by Ritchie Valens and Robert Kuhn
Transcribed by Ryan Sheeler

1. Intro Guitar Lead

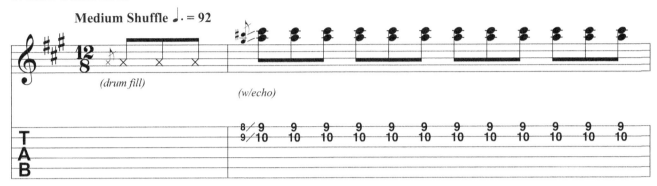

2. Intro Riff (Danelectro and Guitar)

3. Verse Riff / Variation

LITTLE GIRL

4. Bridge Riff

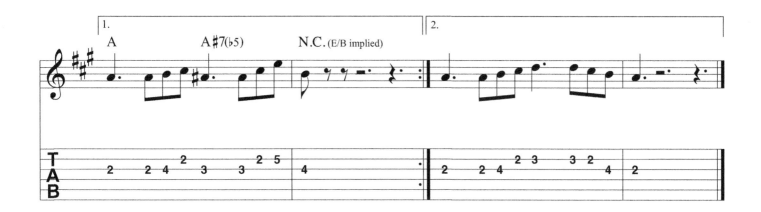

41

Alt: Capo on 1st fret,
play with "E" fingerings:
down 1/2 step

We Belong Together

From the album Ritchie Valens *(1959)*

By Robert Carr, Johnny Mitchell, and Hy Weiss
Transcribed by Ryan Sheeler

Ballad Shuffle ♩. = 69

Verse 1

You're mine ____ and ____ we be - long to -

geth - er, ____ yes ____ we be - long to - geth - er ____

for ____ e - ter - ni - ty. You're

Verse 2

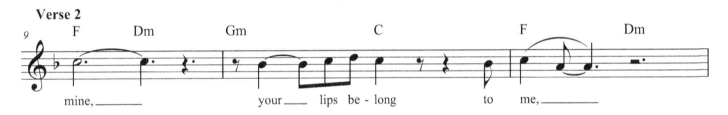

mine, ____ your ____ lips be - long to me, ____

yes, ____ they be - long to on - ly me

for ____ e - ter - ni - ty. You're

Bridge

mine, ____ my ____ ba - by, ____ and

19 F
you'll ___ al - al - al - ways be.   I swear ___ by ___ ev - 'ry -

22 Bbm   G 7
thing I own, ___   you'll al - ways, ___ al - ways ___ be

Verse 1a

24 C   F   Dm   Gm   C
mine. _____ You're mine,   and ___ we be - long   to -

27 F   Dm   Gm   C   F   Dm
geth - er ___   yes, ___ we be - long   to - geth - er ___

30 Gm   C   F   Bb   F   *(Danelectro Bass – freely...)*
for ___ e - ter - ni - ty.

Backstage at the Fiesta Ballroom, Montevideo, MN, January 27, 1959.
Check out his fabulous threads!

Stay Beside Me

From the album Ritchie *(1959)*

Words and Music by
Bill Olofson and Maurice Ellenhorn
Transcribed by Ryan Sheeler

The Paddi-Wack Song

From the album Ritchie *(1959)*

Traditional
Arranged by Ritchie Valens
Transcribed by Ryan Sheeler

Alt: Capo on 1st fret,
play with "E" fingerings:
transpose down 1/2 step

Guitar

Alt: Capo on 1st fret,
play with "E" fingerings:
transpose down 1/2 step

THE PADDI-WACK SONG

From the album Ritchie *(1959)*

Traditional
Arranged by Ritchie Valens
Transcribed by Ryan Sheeler

1. Guitar solo (mm.27–42)

Driving Rock ♩ = 144

CRY, CRY, CRY

From the album Ritchie (1959)

Alt: Capo on 1st fret,
play with "A" fingerings:
down 1/2 step

Words and Music by
Ritchie Valens and Robert Kuhn
Transcribed by Ryan Sheeler

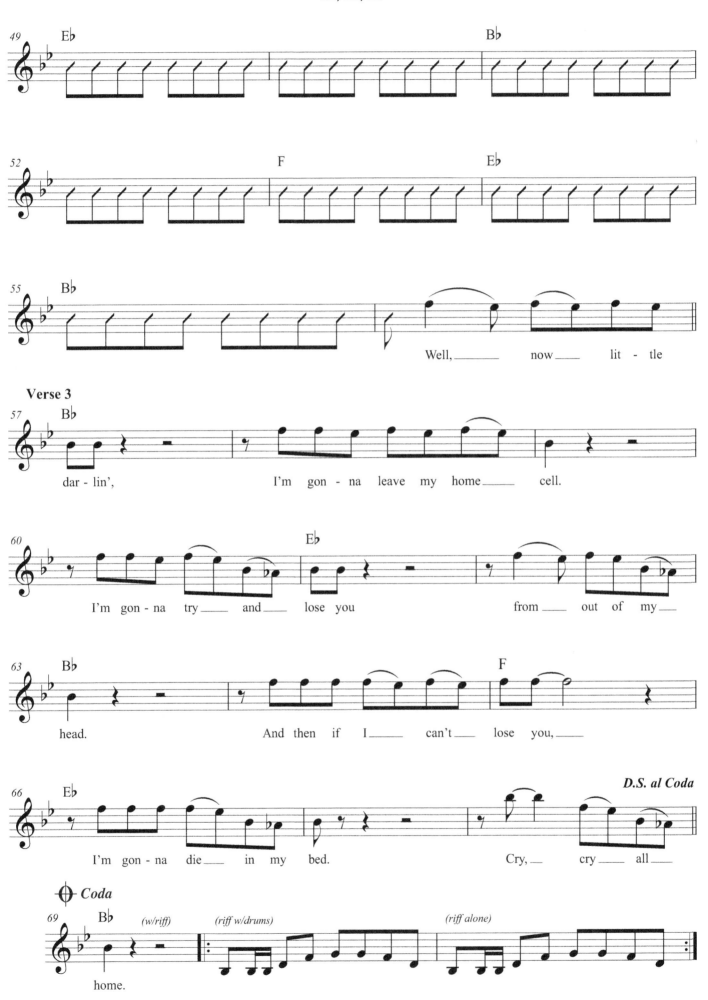

Verse 3

dar - lin',   I'm gon - na leave my home____ cell.

I'm gon - na try___ and___ lose you   from ___ out of my ___

head.   And then if I___ can't___ lose you,___

D.S. al Coda

I'm gon - na die___ in my bed.   Cry, ___ cry ___ all ___

Coda

(w/riff)   *(riff w/drums)*   *(riff alone)*

home.

CRY, CRY, CRY

From the album Ritchie *(1959)*

Alt: Capo on 1st fret,
play with "A" fingerings:
down 1/2 step

Words and Music by
Ritchie Valens and Robert Kuhn
Transcribed by Ryan Sheeler

1. Main riff (intro, verses, etc.)

1b: Main riff in A (capo on 1st fret, sounds in B♭)

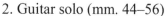

2. Guitar solo (mm. 44–56)

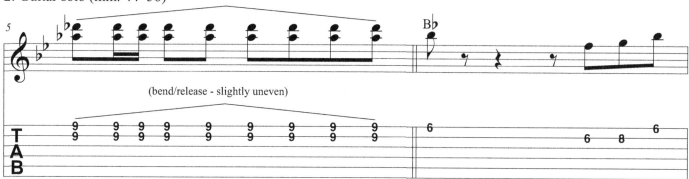

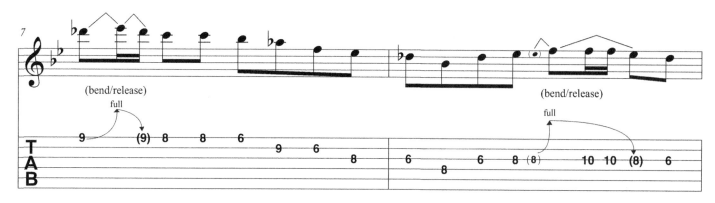

CRY, CRY, CRY

Acknowledgements

Thanks be to God and my Lord and Savior, Jesus Christ—my strength and my song (Psalm 118:14)

My family for supporting and believing in me, especially my parents for instilling in me a love of music.

This project would not have been possible if not for the help and guidance of the following. I am so grateful for your help, your knowledge, and your willingness to share your love of Ritchie and his music.

- Connie Valens and The Valens Family / *Hi-Tone Five, Corp.*
- Ani Khachoian / *C3 Entertainment*
- Ron Middlebrook / *Centerstream Publications*
- Charylu Roberts and Ronny Schiff / *O.Ruby Productions*
- Beverly Mendheim
- Sal Gutierrez
- Gil Rocha
- Carol Kaye
- Gail Smith
- Crystal Jackson
- Jim McCool and Sevan Garabedian / *Blue Days Productions, Madison, WS*
- Sheryl and Sherry Davis / *The Surf Speaks*
- The Iowa Rock 'n' Roll Museum Association and Hall of Fame (IRRMA), Arnolds Park, IA
- The Surf Ballroom, Clear Lake, IA, and everyone in the extended "February Family"/ It is so much fun to join you every year for the Winter Dance Party and share the music and memories.

Bibliography

I. Books

1. Keane, Bob. *The Oracle of Del-Fi*. Del-Fi International Books, 2006.

2. Lehmer, Larry. *The Day The Music Died*. New York: Schirmer Trade Books, 2000.

3. Mendheim, Beverly. *Ritchie Valens: The First Latino Rocker*. Tempe: Arizona State University, Bilingual Review Press, 1987.

4. Reyes, David and Tom Waldman. *Land of a Thousand Dances: Chicano Rock 'n' Roll from Southern California*. Albuquerque: University of New Mexico Press, 2009.

II. Compact Discs, Audio Recordings, and Liner Notes

1. Valens, Ritchie. *Ritchie Valens.* Wounded Bird, 2006.
   (original release Del-Fi Records, 1959).

2. Valens, Ritchie. *Ritchie.* Wounded Bird, 2006.
   (original release Del-Fi Records, 1959).

3. Valens, Ritchie. *In Concert at Pacoima Jr. High*. Wounded Bird, 2006. CD.
   (original release Del-Fi Records, 1960).

4. Valens, Ritchie. *The Ritchie Valens Story*. Del-Fi, 1993.

5. Valens, Ritchie. *Come On, Let's Go!* Del-fi Records, 1998. (CD box set).

6. Various Artists. *La Bamba: Original Motion Picture Soundtrack*. Rhino/Slash, 1987

III. Films and Documentaries

1. *Chicano Rock!: The Sounds of East Los Angeles*. Directed by Jon Wilkman, PBS, 2009.

2. *Go, Johnny, Go!* Directed by Paul Landres, Hal Roach Productions/Valliant Films, 1959.

3. *La Bamba*. Directed by Luis Valdez. Produced by Taylor Hackford. Columbia Pictures, 1987.

4. *Pacoima Stories,* Crystal Jackson Productions. Pacoima, California, 2016.

5. *The Ritchie Valens Story/The Complete Ritchie Valens,* Whirlwind Media, Inc., 2000.

More Great Guitar Books from Centerstream...

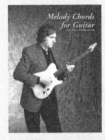

More Great Guitar Books from Centerstream...